The Language of Grief

~

poems by

Alex Gallo-Brown

ISBN: 1-931002-12-7

Cover design by Cathy Brown
Photo by Jennifer Lobsenz

Wordrunner Press
Petaluma, California

for my dad

for Jenne

and for my mom
and the other women in my life
who have encouraged
my breath and voice

And it was at that age…poetry arrived
in search of me. I don't know, I don't know where
it came from, from winter or a river
I don't know how or when,
no, they weren't voices, they were not
words, nor silence,
but from a street it called me,
from the branches of the night,
abruptly from the others,
among raging fires
or returning alone,
there it was, without a face,
and it touched me.

— Pablo Neruda

The need to be rooted in one's environment and, still more, in one's cultural and historical past, is as essential for the soul as roots in the soil are for a plant.

— Richard Rees writing on Simone Weil

Contents

A note on the poems and grief

Inever meant to write grief poems. I never meant to write any poems, in fact. Over the last seven years I have identified as a poker player, a student of creative writing, a restaurant worker, a political Leftist, a caregiver for people with disabilities, a labor organizer, a literary essayist, and an apprentice farmer. Almost never, however, have I identified as a poet. The reasons for this are complicated, I'm sure, not least to do with the paucity of poetry in our culture. (Try telling someone who you have just met that you write poems. Now watch their eyes glaze over with incomprehension and embarrassment.) Mostly, though, I have been reluctant to identify as a poet because I never really felt like one. The version of myself that walks and talks and moves around in the world feels very different from the one who summons poetry.

Nevertheless, the poems have come and continue to come, in bursts of creative energy, like wind gusts, that leave me disoriented on the page. Usually I am surprised at what gets put down there. Sometimes, I am ashamed.

Even still, the poems collected here do, I believe, cohere into something almost resembling a narrative. This is a story, finally, about grief. There are exhortations of love here and gasps of fear, flashes of self-discovery followed by descents into confusion and pain. Apparently I have been grieving for longer than I even knew.

～

When we think about grief, it is usually the intense feelings (shock, melancholy, fear, anger, ebullience, and despair, to name a few) that follow the loss of a loved one to death. And for good reason. Losing a partner, a parent, a friend, or especially a child can be spectacularly painful for those involved.

I would like to take a moment here, however, to complicate such a conception of grief, to expand its definition to include all feelings that result from a dramatic loss in a person's life. We can feel grief when we leave one living situation for another. We can feel it after a longtime partner leaves us—or even after we begin a new relationship (grief for our own lost solitude, in the latter case). We can feel it when our career path changes, or when our values gradually shift (thought, in some cultures, to occur every seven years, the amount of time it takes for a snake to shed its skin, the amount of time it took to write this book). We can feel it when something occurs in our political imaginations, such as after a presidential election, the declaration of a war, or the onset of an economic recession. We can feel it when we are physically or spiritually degraded by our work (grief for our own lost dignity), after we enter a shopping mall (grief for the commodification of our objects), or after we eat a cheap and processed meal (grief for the poverty of our food). In the America I know, grief is omnipresent.

It is particularly troubling, then, that our capacity to talk about grief, to process it in some socially significant way, is as poor as it has ever been. With so few common rituals to turn to, diverted by our innumerable screens, many of us alienated from meaningful labor, and often distant geographically from the people we love, we struggle in the moments of our most urgent loss to recover a language that communicates our lived experience, engaging our individual memories and understanding of our collective history, and that spurs us on to new action, efforts, and creation. Without access to a common language, we find ourselves silent and alone, awash in a commerce bereft of communal context.

This isn't how it has to be. The poems that follow comprise my own raised voice—a shout against the silence.

I

Where our fathers are

My father never left us
so his absence
doesn't haunt me.
Not like Richard Hamilton's shoulders
from that terrible game in '98—
his perfectly held follow-through,
his backwards tumble,
his shorts
screeching across
free throw line,
his shot
arcing over
our giant German center
and through.

Just a month before Hamilton broke
my virgin heart, my father scooped me up
with a voice like arms to show me
the beauty of college basketball.
We huddled outside Hec-Ed
while the night howled at us
to bag it—*go home!* you could hear
it in the wind—but we kept waiting,
hoping cheap tickets would
materialize from the mist.
Finally we got in, middle of the first half,
all of our cash gone,
so we sucked week-old Starbursts
for their moisture.

Later that year
in the biggest game of any of our lifetimes,
Hamilton's shoulders stayed
straight and true
even as the rest of him

caved to the floor
and my father and I yelped
like beaten dogs, ate dinner
in silence.

~

Eight years later, I watch another group of Huskies
saunter onto my TV screen.
They are the same age as me,
most of them.
I wonder where their fathers are.

After the game, the coach will say,
These kids will remember
this game for the rest of their lives.
But he doesn't mention us,
the thousands of hearts and minds
who for months clutched our televisions
to our breasts like they were the arrows of Cupid,
sharp enough to puncture chest bone
if only we rooted hard enough.
Is it our fault they lost?
Did we swallow them up
with how much we wanted them
to remain flesh and blood?

Eight years later,
I bring the television close to my face
like a mirror.
In these new Huskies' faces,
I see us all become ghosts.

~

Nowhere is my father,
heart bleeding in front
of a different set
altogether.

That winter

It was that time of year
when everything goes gray
without warning.
The sky, the ground.
Our skin.

That winter, in our middle school,
rainwater leaked down on us
through holes
that weren't supposed to be there,
the floors grew slick enough
to slide.
For weeks we skidded past
glaring administrators until the city paper
ran a story that made a stink.
But nothing reeked.
In fact, I liked the way it smelled,
like doughnuts a lot of days
swept over from the factory across the street.
And other times like pissed-off city,
like the threat of rain
mixed together
with concrete.

Later, in the even grayer
months, our parents
hosted meetings
in their living rooms.
We could hear them arguing
over the television in low
and controlled tones.
Where are our
tax dollars going?

That winter, in our middle school,
rainwater collected on the rooftops,
dribbled down on us
through holes
that weren't supposed
to be there,
invisible, until
you felt the spray.
We yawned our mouths open
and drank straight from the trickle
as though the water couldn't get in
any other way.

Home in my city

I admit sometimes I
don't know this city
as well as I claim to.
Last year, a thousand miles south,
estranged from seasons
and dazed by sun,
I longed for the gray green
of home.
Now closer, only one hundred miles south,
I sense something cold and hungry
about this forest.
We were never from the forest.
Were you the home
in my city?

On weekends I make the long drive north,
through pockets of mist, fog,
past boxes of people.
I change lanes frequently
to remind myself I exist.
Exiting the freeway I pass the park
where we ate pizza once
and flung a Frisbee that glowed.
I remember the late nights with you,
always dark, the space between us
like fire.
In this city of rain and dark,
where we grew up on school busses,
in city parks, on malt liquor
and clumsy attempts at getting high,
were you my home?

Stopped now
in front of my parents' house,
I am barely able to exit this car,

this box,
afraid the ground will give way
beneath my feet,
that all of it is an illusion
absent your breath.

When you begin to run away

When you begin to run away
sometimes you forget
how fast you actually move.
Sneakers slap like drums,
whole days blur,
time
     fades
         in
     and
         out
slips
as easily
as my hand
into yours,
as your whole body
into mine.
Do you remember
how warm we were?
Our bodies twisted
like your hair
before you had it trimmed.
At some point, we began to run away
like two balloons
drifting
towards the same sun.
Then one of us
(was it you or me?)
caught our own gust,
spiraling in the opposite direction
from the other.

But do you remember
how we used to sleep for hours,
whole afternoons falling victim
to our lethargy?

How when we woke,
our eyes bending to the sudden light,
we would stretch together, barely rested,
all our energy
trapped
between the sheets?
When I closed my eyes
I couldn't tell where I ended
and you began.
I snapped them open again, panicked,
then shut them
once I realized
it didn't matter.

A city that waits

You my home are a city that waits,
a city of transplants and permanent shadow.
Your pace is the faint drumbeat
of a blind man's cane,
the *tap tap* against a jogger's leg
when he emerges from places unseen.

> *But do you remember, man, the winter*
> *it rained about a thousand days in a row?*
> *So many days of uninterrupted drizzle*
> *the national news came calling.*
> *That winter we might have killed*
> *for one sun a month,*
> *evergreens soaked, sidewalks softening*
> *like back when they were young and new,*
> *the clouds become like an umbrella*
> *after awhile.*

You my home are a city that waits,
a city of transplants and permanent shadow.
A city of wilderness and concrete framed
by plants whose names we never knew,
of animals domesticated and driven away,
by the buildings that bloom anew each spring
as immovable as your mountain,
as incontrovertible as your lakes.

> *But do you remember*
> *that time when we were lost*
> *and I said this road must lead somewhere?*
> *And it turned out that somewhere*
> *was an Indian reservation three hours down that road,*
> *some sodden, desolate square of filling station*
> *with a name like a moan?*
> *And do you remember those beautiful brown girls*

whose faces were so young
but who already moved like ghosts?
Do you?

You my home are a city that waits,
a city of transplants and permanent shadow.
A city of white people gathered in privilege
while your limits push farther,
your darker denizens shoved out
into that stunned, limitless neon.
A city of people who acknowledge each other
with only the slenderest of nods
like strangers in an elevator.

But don't you remember the summers
when we graded trails in city parks,
let fatigue punch the ground
in puffs of dust
while the city bared its mountain
and evergreens singed the freeways?
And do you remember the night
when fire roared over the ridge
and we thought we might be imagining it
after all those beers, those joints,
that big, licking fire
like some sexual monster
forcing itself against the night?
When we waded outside
to see what was going on,
the heat butted us back
like a cop's baton.

You my home are a city that waits,
a city of transplants and permanent shadow.
A city of migration and movement,
of transience and constant change.
Your people come from New York and Tacoma,

from Connecticut and California,
from Pittsburgh and Poland,
and we, your first born sons and daughters
run off to flit in sexier places,
we are no different.

>   *But don't you remember the freeways*
>   *where we drove north to gamble*
>   *and east to dance*
>   *in the fizzy spray of twelve packs*
>   *and later south*
>   *where mystery threatened*
>   *to swallow us away?*
>   *Don't you remember?*

You my home are a city that waits,
a city of transplants and permanent shadow.
We grew up somewhere away from you
while you wait and wait
for our return.

Through an airport window

I watch the airplane
that is supposed to be carrying me
above these plains,
over this grass, away
from this scrap
of civilization.
But it is motionless, a knife
across the plains.

> *A week ago at home, a bald man*
> *drove a pair of landscaping shears*
> *through my driver's side window.*
> *I had left my wallet in plain view*
> *on the dash.*
> *Days later I would find crumbs of glass*
> *corralled in my sweatshirt pocket,*
> *embedded into the heels of my boots,*
> *rooted beneath fingernails.*

In this airport overlooking the plains,
there is a man upset, his hair
a neglected shrub
shuddering
in the winds of his anger.
His luggage was lost, was stolen,
is some unknowable where else.
He gestures with his arms, amplifies his voice,
demands the woman behind the desk
share in his frustration.
There are simply too many of you,
she wants to say.
Instead, she calls security.
"I have a customer who is being unruly."

Fifteen minutes after the bald man
bashed my window,
I strolled into the sunlight
to find three cops surrounding my car.
What did I do? *I thought, flexing my knees.*
At that moment, the bald man
was using my debit card to buy a pack
of cigarettes from a nearby smoke shop.

In this airport overlooking the planes,
a thin woman clutches a cell phone
to her face, trying to stay calm
as she discusses alternate travel routes,
rental car agreements, food vouchers.
After she hangs up, she examines
her reflection in the window,
working the antenna
between her teeth.

Two hours after the bald man broke
my car he tried another, slightly larger
purchase at a different university district
smoke shop. But it was too late.
The attempted charge, seventeen dollars
and change, was declined.
I don't know whether he was trying to buy
three packs of cigarettes, a bong, a fancy cigar,
a few sticks of incense and a holder,
or a Bob Marley tee shirt.

Eight hundred miles away
from this airport overlooking nothing,
from this plane paralyzed on its runway,
from the angry man and the hungry woman,
a thunderstorm growls and dances,
segments of trees
career down suburban streets,

clouds descend
the color of scabs.
Still, I am suspended in this stillness,
my plane forbidden to go.

The day after the bald man stole
my window he dumped my wallet
in a place where he knew
someone would find it.
That morning the YMCA clerk
pulling into the gray dawn parking lot
spotted it lying on the ground.
She picked it up.
She brushed off the dirt.
Inside, she checked her database
for my phone number.
I found you, *I hear her say.*

II

My history of violence

1

No anti-epiphany. No sudden
precipice. Just the faint susurration
of complacency, the barely-audible whimper
of poetry leaking out
of my life.
My new life littered
with receipts   floss picks   q-tips
multivitamins   remote controls   ice trays
websites   forms   applications
in need of my name my signature
and suddenly I am feeling very *described*
as Ed Dorn might say.
I am not making excuses here,
it is important
you understand this.

2

She was there
and then she was not
there, an aching hole only
when I gave enough attention
to my life for it to ache.
The sheets are not why I don't sleep—
I've changed them three times this week.
Still, I lie here in this bed empty
besides me, hugging a pillow to my chest
as though the feathers were daggers
with which to murder
awakeness.

3

I know nothing of violence.
Once, when I was fourteen, I shoved
two twelve year-olds (one with each hand!)

into the school gymnasium stands.
They had been messing with my friend
who was on crutches at the time—
indefensible, useless.
He shuffled away while I chased after him,
laughing maniacally.
Another time—this was years later—
I punched a kid after he grabbed my shirt
and we scrabbled for a minute,
wrestling on the floor.
After that, we were closer than before—
we shared a certain bond, a commonality
of experience.
Another time, I hit my head
very hard on the floor
and my eye swelled up so large
kids gasped when I marched by,
searching for my orange juice
colored school bus.
All I wanted was sleep
but they wouldn't allow it,
someone slapped my face
so I would stay.

4

The day I learned my girlfriend
who was not my girlfriend
had fucked a boy in a far-off city
(she, too, in that far-off city),
I drove south on I-5 to gamble on horses.
It was June, eighty degrees, a beautiful
Northwest day,
a kind of divine reward
after enduring all those months
of shitty gray.
At the track, I stood among sheaves
of discarded betting slips,

the air reeking of spilt and stale beer,
and also that beautiful odor of compulsion,
breathing it all in
while I typed terse
and meticulous text messages.
Later, I was calm as I detailed
the precise sexual acts
I had performed with other girls
when I was her boyfriend
but not her boyfriend.
She begged me to stop
but I kept on,
babbling, frightened,
and violent.

5

Lately, I have been less frightened
and still there have been times
when I fled otherwise salubrious meals
with friends (is this a form of violence?),
convinced at any moment
a runaway bus might strike me dead
or that I would suffer some other
absurd and spontaneous death—
my life snuffed out in the amount of time
it takes to swallow a crust of bruschetta.
Isn't it true that the more pleasure
one experiences in life,
the more one begins to fear death?

6

Would you believe me if I told you
this idea comes from no philosopher or poet
but a professional cut man named Cus,
a man who wields gauze and iodine
to staunch the flow of his fighter's blood?

Question poem

*One couldn't help but wondering how so many whimsical, wicked
people could live under such a sky. But this is only a question that
would occur to the very young.*

— Fyodor Dostoyevsky

The first question is what?
Why would only the young
wonder such things?
Whether only the young
are able to retain
such a naked curiosity?
Or is he referring to their misanthropy?
But don't we become more
misanthropic as we age
as we become more exposed
to the wickedness of life?

If you're wicked, aren't I?
Are there no such thing as murderers,
only people who murder?
How about that boy in front of me
yanking his girlfriend's hair out
on this subway platform?
Great tufts of it there
padding the cement?
What about the girl
digging her nails
into the side of his head?
Bitch! she shouts. *Pussy!*
Which one of us
does she mean?

How can that woman laugh
when we still hear that girl's voice
reverberating through this subway tunnel?
What's so fucking funny anyway?
Can't she see how wicked the world is?
Doesn't she know how many of us live
under this bright sky?

One sun

There are constantly…lions in the village,
who walk about without any hindrance at all.
On the condition that we pay no attention to them,
they pay no attention to us.

— Henri Michaux

You remember, man, when it rained
about a thousand days in a row?
So many days of drizzle
the national news came calling.
I don't think I would have noticed, otherwise.
You know how it gets
so you can't feel, anymore?

That February, we might have killed
for one sun a month.
The evergreens soaked, the cement softening
like back when it was young and new,
the clouds become like an umbrella
after awhile.
Man, I know the sound of your clip
clopping windshield wipers by heart.
Your raggedy speakers, too.
So what of you now?
I haven't been gone so long.

All these months you say nothing
yet you tremble.
I feel the vibrations travelled
all the way out here.
Do you think you bear this alone?
When do you speak without disguise?
When have you ever?
I don't say this to wound.
I could say other things.

I'll say just one more now.
Always there will be lions
roaming the village.
But Michaux was wrong—
you ignore them,
they'll snap you up anyhow.
We have here one sun, hear?
And only for a little while.
Time, of course:
one must arrive a little sooner
than it does.

Sunday

At a yard sale,
enough silverware to feed a family of five
costs me two dollars.
Somebody's mother
drops it all into a plastic bag
the steak knives nudging holes
into the sides.
She says she hopes to see me around,
even though she doesn't have to.

At another sale, for a dollar each,
I buy VHS copies
of *Do the Right Thing* and *Reservoir Dogs,*
aware that I own no VHS player
and besides that no TV.

I am optimistic.
You might say I have a gift
for anticipation.

A few blocks down, at a sidewalk café
I pay four times as much
for a poorly conceived
disastrously executed
chicken souvlaki.
I tip the waiter
who calls me buddy
more than I should.

Later, near my apartment,
I sit on the sidewalk writing
within stroking distance
of a municipal sign.
"Danger!" it says. "Men Working Above."
But when I look up
I see no one.

The film starts

in twenty minutes
but already the moviegoers
are crunching contentedly
over their vats of popcorn,
shuffling in on their Sundays,
purses and briefcases rustling.
I leave a buffer seat between
me and the woman with shopping bags
to my right but the beefy man to my left
extends no such courtesy.
We spend a few minutes
watching tense advertisements.

After the film begins,
it's really heavy-handed stuff:
the Individual facing off against
the Oppressive Communist Regime, etcetera.
The Human Spirit is on the verge of triumph,
I can feel it,
when an aging but light-hearted prostitute
with massive breasts makes an appearance.
The audience squirms.
The man to my left guffaws.

She lasts only a few moments on screen
before we are tossed back to our themes.
After the film ends, a certain awkwardness ensues.
Clearly, some here among us would like to launch
into spontaneous and heartfelt applause,
while the rest are ready to move on with our day.
Finally, the spontaneous crowd decides to clap,
although I'm not sure how much heart
they really put in.

Later, it occurs to me that the prostitute
was supposed to symbolize *loneliness.*
But those breasts made it impossible
for her to stand for anything but herself.
Talk about
individuality.

Dollar on the ground

Neither of us wanted to show
we wanted it.
But both of us did.
Finally, I knocked hammer to ice
and scooped the bill from the ground.
"He who hesitates," I said, feeling guilty.
"He who gives, gets back even more," he replied,
doubt flickering in his eyes.

Cruel light

Another morning
waking up with breath
stinking of foolishness,
of hanging around too late
at an apartment with a couple of girls
who looked better than an empty bed
though not better than much else,
still, just hanging around because
inertia beats movement
when you've got nowhere to go.

Colorado sounds nice, but only in theory,
because you've been there before
and sure the mountain flares prettily
outside the window
and the air is sharp enough
to make you really breathe.

But here it's damn cold too,
even with the sun out
and casting its cruel light.
Here it's so cold you can forget
sun used to mean warmth,
so cold that you sprint
from subway to apartment
and back again,
that you sprint
through this glinting cold
like there was something you wanted
on the other side of it,
like you knew where it was
that you were going.

III

One howling syllable

Days
were almost
the same
as before,
different only
in unquantifiable ways,
in fractions
of moments,
the strangeness,
the newness of it
blunted by activity.
Almost any kind
would do—
card-playing,
food-cooking,
eating and more
eating.
We laughed at anything then,
even stupid things
could be funny.
Needed to be.
The laughter
like rain-pour:
slashing
      mindless
          cleansing.
You would give more now.
Life you understood
to be one small exercise
in giving,
death simple cessation
of that ability.

But nights were a different ballgame
played in a foreign park,

their field lights burned to darkness.
At night, the voices grew bold,
forging elaborate dialogues
replete with all
the idiosyncrasies of conversation.
And other times
just that one
howling syllable.

What is happening to us?

So many of his final hours
spent sliding across
the slippery surface
of television.
So many hours spent
turning away
from what was happening.

I don't mean the final hours.
Those were spent in a hospital alone,
in a foreign country looked after by doctors
who spoke nothing of his language,
whose names were so foreign, so frightening,
so ultimately unpronounceable,
he began in phone calls home
to identify them as actors from old TV shows.
Ted Danson administered the tests today,
he might say, *but E.G. Marshall,*
he's the one really in charge.
He did this to make them more familiar,
to vitiate the significance of their threat,
to relegate them to surface.

But I was talking about
before the hospital, before
the doctors.
I was talking about the hours spent
yawning in front of old Westerns,
folding laundry in our TV room,
guffawing along with the canned laughter
of Letterman and Seinfeld.
I meant the hours spent searching
for meaning or something similar
where there was only
a fortress of surface.

I meant the hours spent turning away
from what was happening to him,
from what is happening to all of us
all of the time.

Twinges

Everywhere
there are reminders.
How could there not be?
The alternative
too horrible
to imagine.

The barista bellowing out
his standard order, shrill
amid a coffeehouse
of strangers.

The baseball field
where once we chewed
the spiced skin of fried chicken.
It's the Holy Trinity, I joked,
baseball, chicken, and teenage girls.
I hadn't meant it, of course, not the part
about the girls (in reality I marveled
at how young they looked, how rapid
life was becoming), but it sounded knowing
and tough, as typically masculine
as both of us knew ourselves
not to be.

These twinges
against the larger grief
like the family
doctor telling you
it's only going to hurt a moment
before he jerks the needle in.
And maybe it is that brief—
the coffee whisked from the countertop,
the barista's shout fading
into the voiceless murmur,

the baseball field drifting
across the rearview mirror,
peeling from sight.
But somehow after it's worse.
No one there to warn you,
only the intractability
of every day.

In the peace there were smells

He found he was burying his nose
into things more, itching to get out,
to shove away the screen door
with the edge of his snout,
to rediscover the wind and the plants
and the glory of a night
loosed from its cover.
Food had even begun
to shed some of its luster.
More and more he felt something calling to him,
something unavoidable, humorless to its core.
It was not funny—it had limited capacity
to understand—but there was a softness, too,
a glow irrepressible along
the deserting horizon
of memory.
He had stopped trying
to figure anything out,
and in the halt there was peace
and in the peace
there were smells.
Endless amounts of them.
They might not be here
when he returned.

The language of grief

She says to the dog,
what will you do
without your brother?
This, though I have voiced
no intention of going anywhere.
She means, in this language
she has come to speak,
what will she do without her son?
She means, who will she be
without her husband?
She means, what will we be
when the gasping wind
throws the dust
from our bones?

The ravine

Today, I trotted through the old ravine
with the mutt you may
as well have fathered.
As we went along, I wept,
not because you were gone
but because you weren't here
to see how beautiful
was the day—
sunlight slanting
through slender lacunae
in the canopy, plunging down
through the branches to rain over
our shoulders, brushing our faces
with what was so clearly
kindness.

We didn't stop, me and the dog.
We went on, in fact, right
into the thick of it,
bending our faces towards a sky
that seemed suddenly far away.

Certain in our hurt

Brother, I have feelings
sharp as knives.
They creep up fast sometimes,
mince my mind
into splinters, slice
their sudden blades
through my unexamined flesh.

I never meant to hurt you.
Last night, I wore anger
like another skin.
I held it close to me, hurdled
through its fast burn.
But couldn't you see
how it wasn't so different
from how I've worn joy
in the past, and love?
How it wasn't so different
from the best parts of me,
those precious metals I spent years
drilling deep to find?

Brother, sometimes I feel
strong as a mountain.
Strong enough to keep you standing
while you wail in your hurt.
I feel strong enough then
to heft the whole world's weight—
as a duty of my existence, say,
a payment for life still won.

But there are other times
when what I wouldn't give
to suckle up to some forgiving teat.
To slough off all that weight
like a discarded dream.
And when that teat isn't there?
I still feel like a mountain.
Only then I am liable to explode,
erupt over you and anyone close.

Vantage point

Pedal pressed to the mat,
I catch a glimpse of a new strip
mall as it zips past.
New mall, same landscape,
just another citizen christened
into this land of chain stores,
gas stations, casinos.
Alongside of me tinted faces ride,
alone in their boxes,
praying to the next green light.
No crowds, just cords of cars
connecting Monday and Friday.

As brake lights flash at me
to slow down,
I glance up,
find the eye of a crow
perched atop
a telephone wire.
He isn't going anywhere,
just content among the sky.

As I look up
while he looks down,
I wonder if he recognizes something
in this mess
I miss stranded
in the middle of it.
Maybe, for him, there is geometry
to this traffic, red lights
halting lanes into perfect
squares and rectangles.
Maybe, in his way of looking,
humans tread gently

over this vast earth,
a race in unison.

But how could we ever
get that high?

Warehouse of defeat

The casino was dead air today,
no breath, a warehouse of defeat.
I admit, I joined them
in their weakness.
I think maybe I wanted to feel less
whole, to disperse myself through
those slender circles.
In any case, I played,
was fruitfully scattered.
As I walked out, the security guard
smiled at me, her face tender
yet distraught.
Whose face was that?
Mine?
Were all of us so transparent
in our vacancy?
Outside, I gulped air,
a kind of reverse weeping.
There were casinos for miles
and miles.

Poem to a black dog

Pink tongue,
black bearded body,
how you have kept me sane
these long months
even as your hips sag
beneath my touch,
wilt like sun-baked flowers.
Poor creature, blessed with short memory
and superior sense of smell,
your days must be only negligibly distinct,
a free-flowing fountain
of disorganized time.

Or maybe this is just what we say
to make sense of your seemingly
eventless existence.
Maybe you are actually more
attuned to each day,
to their unpredictable waves,
their subtle surprises.
Maybe you are a food critic
endowed with a nuanced tongue,
a jeweler who examines thousands of diamonds
but not one of them the same.

So that you might taste
that close.
So that you might see
that clear.

Clear light

Papa, let me tell you,
there's nothing quite like
watching the smoke
curl up from the ashtray
in this clear light of mourning.

IV

Chacala

Where the sun setting
can still stop
a human cold

Where the waves lap
against the beach
like a beat cop
making the rounds

Where the sky springs pink
like the cotton candy
of childhood

Where the people stand in silence,
watching the sea
and the sun,
and the dogs sit at peace
with their fleas

Where the blowfish wash up
dying or already dead
and the vultures are greasy black
and hesitant

Where the greasy, hesitant vultures
snack on the dead blowfish

Where the waves never stop

Where the mosquitoes come to visit at night
like old friends
and leave with a little blood
like old friends

Where the geckos cackle
high in the walls
and the snakes keep
mostly to themselves

Where the rats
drown in the toilets
and the wasps always wake
on the wrong side of the nest

Where the scorpions
skitter along the rocks,
afraid to be captured
and preserved
in the plastic key chains
sold to tourists

Where the Mexicans drain
their whales of beer
and the Americans tongue
their strings of cheese

Where things are always changing
the waves keep up their work
and the children are never alone

Red islands

At night here, when I sleep,
mosquitoes flock
from far-away homes
to enter my ankles
with their spear-like straws.
In the mornings, my skin is pocked
by the faint islands
of their evidence.
In the afternoons, the islands itch.
After I scratch them, they hurt.

At night here, when I sleep,
I dream and sometimes remember.
In the mornings, I wake and cry a little.
Yesterday I visited your headstone
for the first time.
The stone was dirty.
Dust had crawled into the cracks.
Your name had faded.

At night here, when I sleep,
sometimes you are there
and everything is as it was before.
In the mornings, I wake and cry a little.
This afternoon I will take a bucket
of soapy water and clean rag
to wash the dirt
from the crevices
of your face.

Reading Octavio Paz in Mexico eighteen months after your death

Eighteen months
like a succession of dreams,
relentless, without respite.
Some of those days spent
thinking about you,
turning the memories over
in my mind,
letting them sift
against my skin.
Other days just hurrying
through the fog.
Nobody thinks about his own death, Paz writes,
because nobody lives a personal life.
But I do, Paz, I do.
I wonder if this is the last bus
I will ever ride, the last bit of earth
I will ever glimpse.
It wouldn't be so hard, would it?
An errant flick of the driver's wrist,
then formless, bodyless,
among the stars.

Eighteen months like a succession
of dreams, relentless
without respite.
Reading Octavio Paz in Mexico
lecture on death, hector
on death, an implacable orator,
an ancient high priest.
You were always more
like a jester, singing lightness
from your corner of the court.
You brought people to you,
you took them in.

Tell me how you died, Paz writes,
and I will tell you who you are.
All right, Paz, I will tell you
how my father died.
On assignment, a travel writer
in a foreign land,
frightened, perhaps, but in love *todavia,*
devout in this faith
until his end.

The company of desire

Fallen angel, inhabiting my bed,
let me say first of all
that I am grateful.
There was a time when I might
have grated against such company,
preferring the clarity of solitude
to all this inscrutable pleasure.
But no more.
You who are soft
like no material I have had cause
to touch, a creature (there is no other
explanation) designed by the divine.

It is very late now.
A gray dawn falls
through the window.
If I were a different man,
or even previous incarnation of same,
I might wake you now
and claim the comfort
of your company.
But no more.
Angel, you sleep now
so that you might take
what you need
from your dreams.

Denier of catastrophe

I am good at making plans,
good at fresh starts.
How many unopened notebooks,
packs of unsharpened pencils?
I would leapfrog states for you,
storm through oceans and beyond.

This afternoon I smoked until my stomach
hurt and sweat beaded my brow.
Later, I paced the apartment naked, sipping
coffee and trying to multiply my attention.
I printed a story I already wrote,
mailed it to an editor who may
or may not exist.
What I really wanted
was to write a story
I hadn't thought of yet,
but that was harder,
so I smoked until my lungs complained
and clicked on things that didn't interest me.

Honey, there is no end for us,
not that I can see.
Call me, if you must,
a denier of catastrophe.
But your body and your body
and your body and—
I stand defiant
in your face.
Baby, let me hold myself
under your roof.

Tiny Mexicans

I fool myself into happy patter.
Tap at plastic keyboard
swing frying pan across stove
slumber briefly among images
of strange and stormy men
then launch back to work
come morning.

But earlier I was in the park
playing basketball with tiny Mexicans.
But earlier I was in the street
swimming in the light
made by gleaming cars.

For forever I have put cigarette ends
in the womb of an ocean shell.
The ocean I have not seen in many moons.
But more of the moon
I have seen than you.

The apartment on Fargo Street

I used to do dirty things, shameful.
Used to gamble my money away,
frequent strip clubs, sleep until noon.
I used to get mad at my friends
and stand in the street shouting.
One night, I tried to convince a car
full of Asian boys to buy me a hamburger
if I gave them the money first.
Their refusal I found unforgivable.
I might have liked to pound
their smooth baby faces
into the parking lot pavement,
bury my head in a stripper's breasts
before stumbling home to sleep.

But this was before I knew you.
This was before we built
the apartment on Fargo Street,
where so much has flowered, gone right,
even if we are poor and sometimes bored.
I sleep most nights now, have forsaken fast food.
An old friend who came to visit recently
told me our apartment felt warm.
But he didn't mean its capacity to retain heat,
the efficacy of our radiators.
He was talking about our hearts,
the way they beat through this place
even when we yell at each other
and threaten to drive hundreds of miles away.
It feels warm in this apartment,
warm in this union,
warm.

Worker's compensation

First,
a mistake.

Your garden
variety carelessness
combined
with the inane desire
to please.

Then a split
in the nail
so quick
it was like it
happened apart
from time altogether.
A bright red rod
scoring the bed
in two.

The immediate reaction
to contain.
To push the nail back together.
To do the thing over.

Not so much pain
as embarrassment.
A sudden descent
into the physical.

∼

The faces in the emergency room
frozen in their grief.
Or else not really grieving.
Come here for a minor procedure.
Faces immobilized
for some other reason.

~

The doctor tells me
since her divorce
she has been listening
to more music now.
She tells me how her nephew
helped her order a stereo online,
how it arrived at the house
in a flurry of boxes.
She tells me how proud she was
of herself for figuring it all out.
But how sad she seemed in herself
for figuring it all out.

~

Wait a few minutes, the sad doctor says.
You won't feel a thing.
Using a miniature pair of scissors,
she cuts away the top of my nail.
Then with a needle and thread,
she sews the skin back together.

Gordon

Someone tells me
the liver regulates fluids,
that when the liver's taxed
the body reacts more easily
to airborne allergens.
This makes a poetic sense to me,
a lyrical sense, even though
my knowledge of anatomy is piss
poor and Wikipedia confounds me.

Ever since, I have been trying to avoid
cheese, to consume less wheat,
to eat vegetables grown
beneath the skin of the soil.
But tonight, perhaps because of stress
and perhaps because it is my job to care
for an elderly disabled man who enjoys
inserting pens into his penis,
I order a pizza and eat it gladly,
all at once, except for the slice
I give to Gordon.
After the hot cheese skins his lip,
I wrap fillets of frozen fish
in paper towels and hold them
against his face.

And where am I now,
now that Gordon has gone to bed?
Fear. Gassiness.
Bloated back, filled with fluids.
Weariness. Stuffy nose.

Jackie

At work today
Denise rolled up her chair
so it clinked with mine
and took a whack
at the back of my head.
Bob keeps promising to have her moved
but everyday she's still there, staring.
It is taking

        so

            long.

At home, I keep the radio
tuned to Christmas songs.
It helps with the silence
that creeps in sometimes,
like the caregiver's hand
during changing time.
It helps with some of it
though not the whole thing.
And anyway, there are commercials.

The organizer's song

Whole days lost
to bad addresses and cold knocks.
To static smiles and queasy imputations.
Son, whyn't you get on?

My job
to remind poor people
the outrage of their circumstance.
My job
to tally the troops.
No one knows I've got a secret
poet living inside me.
No one hears the music
burning me up.

Whole days lost
to this bottomless road.
Abused animal filling my belly.
Ancient plant deposit fueling my tank.
I visit the toothless workers
in their tiny trailers.
The salty coast
decaying their floorboards.
The paper mill spreading smell
all over their country.
Sir, I am so sorry to hear
about your injury.
I have here a card, a flake
of dead tree.
Won't you sign?

The organizer's song II

It's like a little pie, she says.
Have you ever eaten Thai?
The orange juice about the same as before,
the Americano in need of hydration.
I am blessed with a bitter and magnanimous
love, divorced of all history.
Lady, I will visit you in your home.
I will present you with a card.
And I will cry, I will shed
syrupy tears, if you will sign.

Sheridan

Telephone wires drawn tight
against weary sky.
Sky spangled with bright squares
borrowed from some other sky.
I drift through dreary towns
driving the car my dad used to.
Dairy Queen, Wal-Mart, KFC,
you know nothing
of what I have to say.

In Sheridan, I pull to the side of the road
to finish my lukewarm tea.
As I sip, I watch a fat woman deliver the mail.
I watch her fight her own body
just to rid herself of her car.
In the city where I live,
postal workers drive state-issued vehicles.
Here, they use their own.
Hers is a battered jeep, maroon,
a government sign on its roof.
I watch her limp to her first house.
A flag bounces above her
in the wind.
I think I have forgotten
what I have to say.

Holding on

You remember that tea pot
I bought at the thrift shop
down in the southeast?
It was just after we moved
to Portland.
I was driving, aimless,
while you cared for
the neighbor's baby.
Maybe on my way to play
poker, I don't remember.
For two weeks, one month,
I went without telling you.
That pot broke last week.
I flung it against the floor.
You didn't say anything.
You just swept up the shards
and stuck them in the trash.
Later, I fished the top out
and put it on another pot.
I figured you have to hold on
to what you can.

VI

In Dallas

We flash past Dairy Queens
through deserts of green scrub.
I fall asleep dreaming of weeds,
the ache at the end of each day
between thumb and forefinger,
the roots of grass
insistently hanging on,
green beans still new
to this world.

Back in Dallas I saw green beans
like shriveled shoelaces.
I watched an old friend
stomp and sneer at the price
of packaged meat, then swoop
in his bright black car
past glittering buildings
and hulking
corporate headquarters.
In Dallas, I saw self-hate swivel
towards self-love and pivot
back again.

Now ice cream and cattle
and cheap slabs of meat.
Shrubs that look like
they would take whole years
to pull out.

Waiting for espresso

The barista bobs yes,
then turns to work her grinder.
Polka dots slink down
rumpled shorts.
Swaths of skin peek
through gaps in her shirt
like grapes.
She pours my espresso over ice.
A surly taste.

The stranger's car feels, fleetingly,
like freedom.
Tractors litter the countryside
like useless thoughts.
I wait with soured breath
for a leader who might show us
how to live.

In the community I imagine

In the community I imagine,
we will know each other's faces,
trust each other's hands,
grow each other's food.
We will watch each other grow.

In the community I imagine,
some of us will leave to learn external truths
and some of us will return.
Others will abandon, destroy, act out, and violate.

In the community I imagine,
our history will be shared and taught,
argued over and discussed,
and in this way will come to be known.

In the service of love

Intelligence not
in the service of love
is useless at best
and at worst destructive.

Birthday

Father, sixty years ago you came
bluefaced and breathless
into this world,
a brown baby swaddled
in the arms of family.
Today, it is your birthday
but you are not here
and I sit far away
from everything I know
remembering you
(your broad shoulders
and stubby legs)
remembering you
alive.

Father, it feels so good,
      father, it hurts so bad,
          to remember.

Sixty years ago the world opened
and spit you out.
And then you made me.

VII

Dream movie

I can't summon even enough
energy to smash my head
against this wall.
The nice man
sitting next to me
I would puke
into his face. The fuck
wad who raised me
I would break
with my fists.
I am angry even
at my anger.
I wish it was something else
like tenderness
or joy.

The waitress avoided me.
The blackjack table indifferent.
And where was I?
Some fog, some poisonousness,
chowing through Chinese food,
infinite, pathetic.
The limpid broccoli. The lukewarm pork.
Even my tongue, these days, is numb.

Baby, your pain stabs at me,
steals my rationed breath.
I stuff it down. I pack it in.
Our days are blurry and food-filled.
I am at a casino
and then a train station.

I guess I might like to know truth
although not exclusively,
steeped as I am in dreaming

and forgetfulness.
I guess I might like
to leap off dream buildings
like Leo DiCaprio in that movie
I watched while you were in class
about the possibility of release
and insurmountable grief.

You don't know

You said my poems don't go like
you are the stars and moon
and *mother goose,* they don't rhyme,
they're not ooze. Which is true.
But then you said, *they're not about me.*
Not about you?
On the London tube, you tell me,
I'm not good enough for you.
Making a joke, or pretending to.

You forget I am the Other
you study in classrooms
but can never climb inside.
No matter how much we
mount each other, hold
each other, suck each other,
no matter how much we—
you can't know the subjects
of my poems, can't know
how I look at you.
You can't know
how I would extract
the venom of your sorrow
with my teeth, if I could,
how I would spit
it onto the crusted sidewalk,
then cradle you, heft you, boost you.
You don't know what I would do
so not to lose you.

I like you when you're quiet

after Pablo Neruda

I like you when you're quiet.
Riding the subway with me, or the metro
or whatever they call it here,
your eyes the almonds I chop for oatmeal
on our sleepy mornings in Ushaw Moor,
your skin that same color, oatmeal,
or almonds,
or probably paler now
since it is winter
and we have stayed inside
for so long.

We say that we are healing,
dealing with our mysterious pain.
The pain of the common
place. The pain of the everyday.
The pain of growing older.
The pain of incessant change.
The pain of being raised.
The pain that keeps us quiet,
riding underground trains
in famous cities
where no one knows our names.

I like you when you're quiet.
Your almond eyes, your pale skin.
We say that we are healing,
dealing with our mysterious pain.
Your face leaning against glass.

The magazine

Trains have always soothed me.
Or movement has.
I think of the car rides
my father used to take me on
when I was young and feeling fussy,
driving towards nothing,
no destination
but my better mood.
So it is with fathers. Or good ones.
I was lucky.
He took me on real trips, too,
to Vancouver, Montana, and Mexico.
"La cuenta, por favor," I learned to say early,
feeling the pride flush his oaken face.
He looked full of flavor and love
and probably some astonishment, too,
that the movement of his pen
could bring us here,
to this beachy, sun-washed place,
where his son could order in another language
a bill that he would never have to pay.

The magazine meant trips to San Francisco
to fire miniature grenades at the ground
and seclude slender ninja swords
from plastic sheathes.
It meant fortune cookies and fancy meals
and afternoon walks on the beach.
But it also meant mornings soaked in stress,
breakfasts with women whose smiles
made you feel grubby and unwanted.
It meant arguments with himself out loud,
stopping only to instruct me, next time,
to eat my bacon with a knife and fork.
It meant egotist editors chopping his best lines.

It meant puffy promo pieces he preferred
eschew his name.

Mostly, though, the magazine meant movement,
release from the dogged domesticity of home
into a bright and bursting unknown.
It was his car ride to nowhere
but a place you don't yet know,
somewhere new and weightless
and entirely without fear.

Moratorium

after Frank O'Hara

Don't call me father,
wherever you are.
I have grieved you enough
now, I believe I deserve
a reprieve.
I have grieved you
with my body, father.
The Chinese believe grief
afflicts the lungs
and with experience I am
inclined to agree.

The night wakes me with
its oceanic emptiness.
The air resists my advances.
I am an old man
with watery lungs.
No, I am twenty-six years old
and a beautiful woman loves me
and I have enough money
to subsist for a while.
I carry myself through these streets
with a sort of easy confidence.
The people, with their sordid faces,
do not concern me.
It is the night I worry about.
It is the air.

The bridge

Walt, brother, you would hate it here.
It would spoil even your
ineradicable good cheer.
Pound, you'd be pissed, heartbroken,
determined to destroy.
I am not determined.
A milky current flows through me.
Wandering a bridge, I watch tourists
watching a watchtower.
The people here must have great faith
to endure such desecration.
They must believe in their city truly
to defile it so.
I yearn for such faith but am afraid.
My home is so fragile, so rootless,
it almost isn't there.

I wander a bridge, look up at a castle.
I breathe in and am revitalized.
A mother and daughter pass me
holding hands.
A woman brushes hair
out of her lover's face.
I am him
and I am her
and below us the river surges
with possibility.

Coda

Succession

1

My father used to tell me
how he would sit
on his grandfather's lap
and watch the fights.
How riding home from the pizzeria
on cold Connecticut evenings
the hot cheese would heat his knees
through the cardboard,
where the pizza would stay
unless he wanted a face
full of his father's hand—
whap! Quick
and painful.
Another story went that a member
of his family was connected.
An uncle, it might have been.
It was only after his friends
were better educated,
possessed of sufficient irony,
and Scorcese had made all of those movies,
that my dad could brag about
his tangential Mafia ties.
At the time I imagine it was a little scary.
I can't say for sure.
I was born on a different coast.
On television, Italians carried guns,
discharged movie poetry
in rapid, profane bursts.
Sunday nights the Sopranos
reserved our house.
My Jewish mother served spaghetti
to our ghost-skinned guests.
My father and I, we were the only Italians.

2

My great-grandfather loved
to watch the fights.
This fact encompasses everything
I have ever known
about the man—
an intransigent interest
in watching other men
club each other bloody.
The fights were, I imagine,
a story without subtitles
or need of translation:
the junction of fist with body,
the jarred face,
the two men performing
their ancient dance,
pummeling each other for prestige
and power.

3

Actually, I know one other thing.
After they left Italy,
my great-grandparents passed through Ellis Island
before settling in Connecticut.
I imagine them cold, hungry, torn by wind.
I can't say for sure.
How could I?
I was born a hundred years later,
on a different coast altogether,
to a family intent on forgetting.

4

Their son, my grandfather, my father's father,
spoke five languages, Italian included,
but would hear nothing
but English in his house.
Once, I watched a TV movie

where an olive oil salesman
squeezed olives into a jar.
It was a joke, of course, satire of early Coppola,
but this is sometimes how I imagine
my great-grandfather.
Not his son, who was educated by Jesuits,
who ate everything American
except on special occasions.
Waffles for breakfast, tuna fish for lunch.
My grandfather voted Republican
until the day he died.
When my dad turned twenty,
he ran off to another coast
to grow his hair long
and smoke as much weed
as he liked.
I was raised among hippies,
communitarians, Swedes.

5

Once every year around Christmas,
we used to visit my grandfather.
In his youth, he had almost become a priest.
It took him years to return to the Church.
My dad grew up an atheist.
Anything God made him uncomfortable.
In college, after I discovered Buddhism,
I mailed home a book called *Transformation & Healing*.
A year later, I found it on his bookshelf,
crisp, clean, clearly unread.
When I was fifteen, my grandfather told me a story
about working his butt off in Palestine,
studying so as to never get laid.
At least, that's what I took from the conversation.
A couple of years later, he died of colon cancer.
He held on for far longer than anyone
had expected.

Outside his hospice, thousands of insects glowed,
brilliant and strange, against the mountainous
Midwestern dusk.
We never learned their name.
Years earlier he had moved from Connecticut to Iowa.
It's a long story.

6

My family is dying.
What I mean is
there are less of us
than there used to be.
My grandparents raised five children
on frozen waffles, Catholicism, and Eisenhower.
Three of them ended up on the West Coast
with hair like girls
reeking of smoke and rebellion.
The fourth moved to Brooklyn to live
with her wife among Puerto Ricans.
Only the fifth played by his rules.
Two kids, opposite sex spouse,
Jif in the cupboards, white bread on the counter.
My cousins still live there.
Iowa.
One of them works the graveyard shift
at a corporate lab, measuring
the cholesterol content of packaged foods.
Sometimes, when I imagine him,
I think of that guy from the TV movie
squeezing olives into a jar.

7

I was born on a separate coast.
Once, on Christmas, I saw my grandfather.
He was watching football in a big, soft chair.
He used to cheer for the University of Connecticut.
Now he rooted for Iowa and their Hawkeyes.
I didn't ask how he had so seamlessly made the switch.

How he could be living one life on one coast
and then auto dealerships for miles
and fruit an endangered commodity.
Where are all the Italians? I wondered,
watching him watch the game
with silent, studious interest.
My life is full of these TV shows, movies,
adopted stories. When I was born
they tell me I did not want
to leave my mother.
That the doctor hooked forceps
into my face and forcibly yanked me
into this world. That for weeks
my skull bore purple marks.
My dad used to tell me
he thought I was ruined.
But I came forth. I survived.
But here I remain.

Acknowledgments

Thank you to Valerie Trueblood, Randy Joseph and others who have given these poems attention over the years.

Thank you to the numerous Kickstarter contributors who made the publication of this book possible.

And thank you to Jennifer Miran Lobsenz, my love, my life, for always keeping two feet on the raft.

About the Author

Alex Gallo-Brown was born and raised in Seattle, Washington, and studied creative writing at the Pratt Institute in Brooklyn, New York. His essays have appeared in *The Rumpus.net, Salon.com, Bookslut, The Brooklyn Rail,* and *The Collagist,* among other publications. His poems have appeared almost nowhere. This is his first book.